Florida-Backroads-Travel.com

FLORIDA CARPENTER GOTHIC CHURCHES

First Edition 2016

Mike Miller

TABLE OF CONTENTS

INTRODUCTION

Florida Carpenter Gothic churches preserve the best of the state's history and make great destinations for Florida day trips. Most of the churches are still active and welcome visitors for Sunday service, and many have open doors during the week for the convenience of visitors.

Wikipedia lists 36 Carpenter Gothic churches in Florida, and **FLORIDA CARPENTER GOTHIC CHURCHES** has a photograph of each one along with basic information on denomination and date of construction. We also include 3 additional churches that are not on the Wikipedia list but we believe have Carpenter Gothic heritage.

There is a location map in the beginning of the book that shows the locations of the churches discussed in this book.

Carpenter Gothic is a style of architecture that involves architectural details on wooden structures that try to replicate features that were originally carved in stone. In the early days, Florida had plenty of timber – including durable Southern pine – and also an abundance of house carpenters. The style takes advantage of the skills of local designers and carpenters and quite often results in charming and nostalgic structures at far less cost than stone or masonry structures.

The churches in this book are organized by the location of the towns where they are located. Most Carpenter Gothic churches in Florida were built between 1870 and 1900. Some sources indicate there may have been as many as 80 of these churches across the state at one time.

Among the features typical of Carpenter Gothic architecture are lancet windows and doors. These are tall narrow openings with a pointed arch at the top making it resemble a lance. It is also common in Florida to see board and batten siding on these churches and pointed stained glass windows. The churches were built using local wood including pine and cypress. Most of the Carpenter Gothic churches in Florida were Episcopalian.

When you look at the church location map you will quickly realize that most of these old churches are in the northern regions of Florida. Florida's development in the Civil War area began in north Florida where the people were.

The book also has a small section on **Other Historic Churches** that may not fit into any particular architectural category, but which are interesting and take you back into Florida history when churches were the center of community life. There are literally hundreds of such churches in Florida and we are only scratching the surface with the five that we discuss in this book. Future editions will include more of these other historic churches.

Enjoy your visit to a Florida Carpenter Gothic church.

MAP OF CHURCH LOCATIONS

We discuss 39 Carpenter Gothic Churches in this book, and also have pages for 4 churches of special interest that are not classified as Carpenter Gothic.

The map below shows the locations of all of these churches.

ALTAMONTE SPRINGS
Altamonte Chapel

825 E. Altamonte Drive
Altamonte Springs, Florida

Altamonte Chapel was built in 1885 on Lake Brantley, 4.5 miles from its current location. The first settlers who attended the church when it was at Lake Brantley went broke when the 1895 freeze destroyed their citrus groves. The church sat abandoned and went back to the original landowner. He made a deal with Rollins College to get free tuition for his two daughters. Rollins sold it in the early 1900s to two men who dismantled it and hauled it by wagon to the new community of Altamonte Springs. Altamonte Chapel is a member of the United Church of Christ.

AVON PARK
Episcopal Church of the Redeemer

20 East Pleasant Street
Avon Park, Florida

The Episcopal Church of the Redeemer was built in 1894, and is listed in "A Guide to Florida's Historic Architecture. Although the congregation is still active, they meet in a different location in Avon Park.

CITRA
Citra Methodist Episcopal Church South

2010 Northeast 180th Street
Citra, Florida

Photo by Ebyabe

The Citra Methodist Episcopal Church was built in 1881 and is on the U.S. National Register of Historic Places. Citra is on U.S. 301 north of Ocala and is near the former home of writer Marjorie Kinnan Rawlings in Cross Creek. The church is also known as the Citra United Methodist Church.

CITY POINT (COCOA)
City Point Community Church

3783 North Indian River Drive
Cocoa, Florida

The City Point Community Church overlooks the Indian River Lagoon north of Cocoa. It is currently being used as the Brevard County Environmental Field Station. The historic building was built in 1885 and is on the U.S. National Register of Historic Places.

The church has served many purposes over the years. It was originally built as a public hall, school and non-denominational church for blacks and whites. Many surnames of the founders are still prominent in Brevard County: Norwood, Hatch, Sanders, Sharpe, Holmes and Chester. The church was also the seed structure for a host of other churches that relocated when the congregations got too large. Among them are the United Methodist Church of Cocoa, Church of Christ, Church of God, Primitive Baptist Church, Calvin Baptist Church, Indian River Baptist Church, Baptist Enterprise Church and First Apostolic Temple.

DEFUNIAK SPRINGS
St. Agatha's Episcopal Church

144 Circle Drive
DeFuniak Springs, Florida

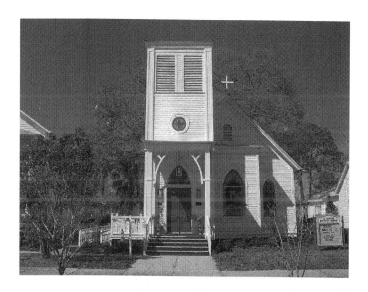

Photo by Ebyabe

St. Agatha's is one of the many properties in the DeFuniak Springs Historic District. It is on Circle Drive, the road that goes around Lake DeFuniak, one of the most perfectly circular lakes in Florida. The church was built in 1896, and has required extensive repairs over the years and was rededicated in December 2007 after restoration work was completed from 2000 to 2007. This church has the only pure pipe organ in the county, built by hand by a member of the congregation and installed in 1990. Although still an active Episcopal church, it is lightly attended.

DUNEDIN
Andrews Memorial Chapel

1899 San Mateo Drive
Dunedin, Florida

Photo by Ebyabe

Andrews Memorial Chapel was built in 1888 and is located at the entrance to Hammock Park in downtown Dunedin. It is listed on the National Register of Historic Places, and has open house on Thursday from 1000am-100pm and Sunday from 200pm-400pm. The chapel is operated by the Dunedin Historical Society.

ENTERPRISE
All Saints Episcopal Church

155 Clark Street
Enterprise, Florida

Photo by Ebyabe

All Saints Episcopal Church was founded in 1881 and opened for worship in 1885. It is listed on the U.S. National Register of Historic Places. Enterprise is a historic village that in the old days was the terminus of navigation on the St. Johns River. Boats would unload their passengers and freight here for shipment via railroad to the coast at Titusville.

FORT GEORGE ISLAND
St. George Episcopal Church

10560 East Fort George Road
Fort George Island, Florida

Photo by Ebyabe

St. George Episcopal Church is located on Fort George Island north of Jacksonville and across the St. Johns River from Mayport. The church was completed in 1883, and was designed by Fernandina Beach architect Robert S. Schuyler. It is on the U.S. National Register of Historic Places.

FORT MEADE
Christ Episcopal Church

331 East Broadway
Fort Meade, Florida

Photo by Indietop20

Christ Episcopal Church is on the U.S. National Register of Historic Places. It was built in 1889.

Fort Meade is an historic old town. It was settled during the Seminole Wars as an Army fort in 1849 on the old military road that ran from Tampa to Fort Pierce. It was originally called Fort Clinch but renamed for Lt. George Meade. Meade went on to greater fame as a Union civil war general who beat Robert E Lee at Gettysburg. Another famous general – a Confederate one - Stonewall Jackson, served at the fort in 1851.

FRUITLAND PARK
Holy Trinity Episcopal Church

2201 Spring Lake Road
Fruitland Park, Florida 34731

Holy Trinity was constructed in 1888. It was built on a one acre lot purchased from a freed slave, Samuel J. Tanner, for $20. The original building had a bell tower but after several lightning strikes and a bat infestation, the church removed it in 1925. The church is on the National Register of Historic Places.

GREEN COVE SPRINGS
St. Mary's Episcopal Church

400 St. Johns Avenue
Green Cove Springs, Florida

Green Cove Springs was a popular tourist destination back in the 1870s, and the chapel was originally built to serve the seasonal guests. The church was built in 1879. A unique feature was the stained glass windows that were made at Colgate Studio in New York City. The church has been recently restored and is on the U.S. National Register of Historic Places.

HAINES CITY
St. Mark's Episcopal Church

109 North 9th Street
Haines City, Florida

St. Mark's Episcopal Church was built in 1890 and is on the U.S. National Register of Historic Places.

HIBERNIA (FLEMING ISLAND)
St. Margaret's Episcopal Church

6874 Old Church Road
Hibernia, Florida

Hibernia is not far north of Green Cove Springs on Fleming Island. The church was built on another site in 1878 and moved to its present location in 1880. The church and its adjacent cemetery are on the National Register of Historic Places. The chapel is among the five oldest wooden churches still standing and operating in Florida although it is no longer an Episcopal church.

JASPER
First United Methodist Church

405 Central Avenue S.W.
Jasper, Florida

The church was built in 1878 and is on the U.S. National Register of Historic Places. Jasper is about halfway between Tallahassee and Jacksonville and almost to the Georgia border.

JENSEN BEACH
All Saint's Episcopal Church

2377 N.E. Patrician Street
Jensen Beach, Florida

This church was built in 1898 on Crossroads Hill in Waveland, now part of Jensen Beach. It's the oldest church building in Martin County. The church is listed in "A Guide to Florida's Historic Architecture" published by the University of Florida Press.

LAGRANGE
LaGrange Community Church

1575 Old Dixie Highway
Titusville, Florida

The original LaGrange Community church was started in a two story log school built on this same site in 1869. The wood frame church of today was built in 1883 and is adjacent to the LaGrange Cemetery. The cemetery contains the graves of many of north Brevard County's earliest pioneers, including Colonel Henry Titus, the namesake of nearby Titusville. Other family names include Norwood, Feaster, Cuyler, Warren and Singleton.

LAKE CITY

St. James Episcopal Church

2425 SW Bascom Norris Drive
Lake City, Florida

The church was built in 1880, but was moved in 1898 to a more convenient site and again in 1987 to a site about four miles away.

LEESBURG
St. James Episcopal Church

204 N. Lee Street
Leesburg, Florida

St. James Episcopal Church was built in 1889 and initially had 157 members. Much of the interior of the original church was destroyed by fire in 1947. The church was rebuilt in 1948 incorporating the original alter and using photographs of the original stained glass windows to make duplicates. So this is sort of an original Carpenter Gothic church, but not quite if one wants to be very strict about the definition. I prefer to look at it, enjoy the atmosphere and relax in the wonderful courtyard garden.

LONGWOOD
Christ Church

151 West Church Avenue
Longwood, Florida

Christ Church is in the Longwood Historic District and was built in 1882. It was badly damaged by Hurricanes Charlie, Francis and Jean in 2004 but has been repaired to its original condition. The church is a member of the Episcopal Diocese of Central Florida.

LYNN HAVEN
First Presbyterian Church

810 Georgia Avenue
Lynn Haven, Florida

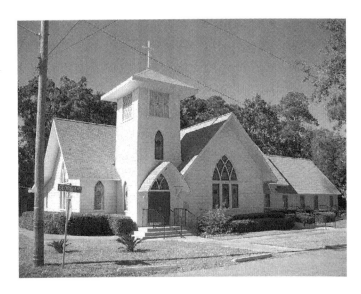

Photo by Ebyabe

First Presbyterian Church of Lynn Haven was built in 1911. It is listed in "A Guide to Florida's Historic Architecture" published by the University of Florida Press.

MADISON

St. Mary's Episcopal Church

108 NW Horry Street
Madison, Florida

Photo by Ebyabe

St. Mary's is on the U.S. National Register of Historic Places. It was constructed in 1881.

MAITLAND
Church of the Good Shepherd

331 Lake Avenue
Maitland, Florida

Photo by Ebyabe

The Church of the Good Shepherd was built in 1880. It was designed by a well-known New York Architect, Charles C. Haight. The church is on the U.S. National Register of Historic Places.

MANDARIN
Church of Our Saviour

12236 Mandarin Road
Mandarin, Florida

The original church was built in 1883 and was attended by Calvin E. Stowe and his famous wife Harriet Beecher Stowe, the author of Uncle Tom's Cabin. Hurricane Dora blew down a huge live oak tree in 1964 and virtually destroyed the old church. The Stowe Memorial stained glass window, created by Louis Comfort Tiffany, was totally destroyed. The congregation built a new church in a design similar to the original.

MELBOURNE
Holy Trinity Episcopal Church

50 West Strawbridge Avenue
Melbourne, Florida

Holy Trinity was built in 1886. The church was originally located on the south bank of Crane Creek, but was moved north of the creek in the 1897. In the 1950s a new church and other buildings were built on Strawbridge Avenue, and the old church became the chapel. The chapel was moved again in 1963 to its present location.

MELBOURNE BEACH
Melbourne Beach Community Chapel

501 Ocean Avenue
Melbourne Beach, Florida

The local residents built the chapel in 1892 and made it non-denominational. It remains that way today. It is on the U.S. National Register of Historic Places.

MELROSE
Trinity Episcopal Church

204 State Road 26
Melrose, Florida

Trinity was constructed in 1886 by a local carpenter, E.L. Judd, who followed a designed based on the work of noted architect Richard Upton. Except for its glass windows and brick foundation piers and chimney, the church is built entirely of local pine, with both inside and outside battens.

MERRITT ISLAND
Old St. Luke's Episcopal Church

5555 North Tropical Trail
Merritt Island, Florida

St. Luke's is in the old area of North Merritt Island known as Courtenay. The church was built in 1888 and both it and its adjacent cemetery are in the U.S. National Register of Historic Places. It is called "Old St. Lukes" to distinguish it from a new church that was built in 1978 next to the old one.

MCINTOSH
McIntosh Presbyterian Church

5825 Avenue F and corner of 7th St
McIntosh, Florida

The church was built in 1907. It is listed in "A Guide to Florida's Historic Architecture" published by the University of Florida Press. The church is a contributing property in the McIntosh Historic District.

MIDDLEBURG
Middleburg United Methodist Church

3925 Main Street
Middleburg, Florida

The church is on the U.S. National Register of Historic Places. Until recently the church was called Black Creek Methodist-Episcopal Church of Middleburg. It was reportedly built by Black slaves in 1847 who also carved the pews. The church had a wide aisle separating the women from the men and the two back pews were for Black members of the congregation.

MILTON
St. Mary's Episcopal Church

6849 Oak Street
Milton, Florida

St. Mary's was built circa 1875-1888 and is listed in "A Guide to Florida's Historic Architecture" and in Frank Lloyd Wright's book "The Aesthetics of American Architecture". Wright wrote **"Saint Mary's is a jewel created in the purest tradition of the Gothic Revival. It survives today with its pure lines intact, its muted colors untouched. Purity, it is without a blemish."** The church is on the U.S. National Register of Historic Places.

MONTICELLO

Christ Episcopal Church

425 North Cherry Street
Monticello, Florida

Photo by Ebyabe

Christ Episcopal was built in 1885 to replace a previous building which burned down in 1883. The building is a contributing property in the Monticello Historic District and is on the U.S. National Register of Historic Places.

OCOEE
Ocoee Christian Church

15 South Bluford Avenue
Ocoee, Florida

Ocoee Christian Church May 2012

Ocoee Christian Church was built in 1891 and is on the U.S. National Register of Historic Places. It is affiliated with the Christian Church and is believed to be the oldest church of that denomination in continuous use in Florida.

PORT ORANGE
Grace Episcopal Church

4100 Ridgewood Avenue
Port Orange, Florida

Grace Episcopal Church was built in 1893 and the Guild Hall was built in 1897. Both buildings are on the U.S. National Register of Historic Places.

PALATKA
St. Mark's Episcopal Church

200 Main Street
Palatka, Florida

Photo by Ebyabe

St. Mark's was built in 1854 and is the oldest church in Palatka. During the Civil War the church was occupied by Union soldiers who caused a lot of damage to the structure. The church is on the U.S. National Register of Historic Places.

SATELLITE BEACH
Holy Apostles Episcopal Church

505 Grant Avenue
Satellite Beach, Florida

Holy Apostles was built in 1902 in Fort Pierce, some 60 miles to the south of its present location. The church was barged up the Indian River Lagoon in 1959 to the then two year old city of Satellite Beach. After being off loaded from the barge, the church was pulled from the river by a bulldozer over telephone poles laid on the ground to act as rollers.

STARKE

St. Mark's Episcopal Church

212 North Church Street
Starke, Florida

St. Mark's was built in 1880 and originally located 20 miles south in the community of Fairbanks. It was called All Saints Episcopal Church back then. Hard freezes in the 1890s wiped out the citrus industry in Fairbanks and church membership plummeted. The church was finally closed in 1890 and in 1900 it was moved to its present location in Starke. The church is listed in "A Guide to Florida's Historic Architecture" published by the University of Florida Press.

TALLAHASSEE
St. Clement's Chapel

815 Piedmont Drive
Tallahassee, Florida

St. Clement's Chapel is also known as St. Clement's Chapel of the Church of the Advent. It was originally built in 1890 in the village of Lloyd in Jefferson County 15 miles east of Tallahassee. It was known than as St. Clement's Episcopal Church. The church structure and membership declined over the years and finally in 1958 the church was deactivated. In 1959 it was given to the Church of the Advent in Tallahassee, moved to its present location and renovated. It was rededicated on November 29, 1959. The church building still has all of its original interior furnishings.

TAVARES
Union Congregational Church

302 St. Clair Abrams Avenue
Tavares, Florida

Union Congregational Church was built in 1888 on land donated by the founder of Tavares, Major Alexander H. St. Clair Abrams. The church is listed in "A Guide to Florida's Historic Architecture" published by the University of Florida Press.

TITUSVILLE
St. Gabriel's Episcopal Church

414 Pine Avenue
Titusville, Florida

St. Gabriel's was built in 1887 and is on the U.S. National Register of Historic Places. It is across the street from the historic Brevard County courthouse. The church was built on land donated by Mary Titus, the widow of Col. Henry Titus, the founder of Titusville.

OTHER HISTORIC CHURCHES

AVON PARK
Union Congregational Church

106 N. Butler Avenue
Avon Park, Florida

The church had its first service on September 11, 1892. It was built on land donated by Oliver Martin Crosby, one of the founders of Avon Park. The church is listed in "A Guide to Florida's Historic Architecture" published by the University of Florida Press.

COCONUT GROVE
Plymouth Congregational Church

3400 Devon Road
Coconut Grove, Florida

Plymouth Congregational Church was built on land donated by George Spalding and George Merrick. Merrick was the founder of Coral Gables. The church was completed in 1917. It was built single handedly by Felix Rebom, who used only a hatchet, a trowel, a plumb line and a T-Square.

FEDERAL POINT
St. Paul's Episcopal Church

130 Commercial Avenue, East Palatka
Federal Point, Florida

St. Paul's was built in 1883 in this rural location not far north of East Palatka on the St. Johns River. The church door is left open during weekdays so visitors can enjoy the solitude inside. Kayakers are welcome to launch their kayaks at SR207 on Deep Creek and use the church's dock on the St. Johns River.

More than 100 years ago Federal Point was a bustling little community with a wharf on the river that was a stop for steamboats out of Jacksonville. The village had a post office, school and small hotel. Nothing much remains of those days except for the church.

MERRITT ISLAND

Georgianna United Methodist Church

3925 S. Tropical Trail
Merritt Island, Florida

Photo by Ebyabe

Georgianna United Methodist Church was built in 1886 in the Georgianna community of south Merritt Island. In 1998 the building was struck by a BMW and knocked 12 inches off its foundation. The building was repaired and is in excellent condition today. Georgianna remains a very active church. Its adjacent cemetery, known as Crooked Mile Cemetery, is the resting place for many Merritt Island pioneers. Although this church is just as old as many of the Carpenter Gothic churches in Florida, it is missing the elements that identify such a church. It has no narrow pointed stain glass windows, for example.

ST AUGUSTINE
Memorial Presbyterian Church

36 Valencia Street
St. Augustine, Florida

Photo by Ebyabe

Henry Flagler was the pioneer who built hotels in St. Augustine and extended his railroad all the way down Florida's east coast until he finally reached Key West. He built this church in 1889 and dedicated it to his daughter Jennie Louise Benedict who died from childbirth complications the same year.

The magnificent church was designed by Carrere and Hastings of New York in the "Second Renaissance Revival" style inspired by St. Mark's Basilica in Venice. The unique construction method used poured concrete mixed with local crushed coquina. The same technique was used to build the Casa

Monica Hotel, the Ponce de Leon Hotel and the Alcazar Hotel. Many of the architectural details were created using terra cotta.

When Henry Flagler died in 1913 He was interred in a marble mausoleum inside the church next to his daughter Jennie Louise and her baby Marjorie, as well as his first wife, Mary Harkness Flagler.

EPILOGUE

Mike Miller has lived in Florida since 1960. He graduated from the University of Florida with a degree in civil engineering and has lived and worked in most areas of Florida. His projects include Walt Disney World, EPCOT, Universal Studios and hundreds of commercial, municipal and residential developments all over the state.

During that time, Mike developed an understanding and love of Old Florida that is reflected in the pages of his website, **Florida-Backroads-Travel.com**. The website contains several hundred pages about places in Florida and things to do. The information on the website is organized into the eight geographical regions of the state.

FLORIDA CARPENTER GOTHIC CHURCHES is based on information in the website written by Mike after visiting many of the churches included in this book, supplemented by information from Wikipedia and from the Fall 2012 issue of The

Florida Historical Quarterly published by the Florida Historical Society.

If you find any inaccuracies in this book, including churches that no longer exist, please contact Mike at **Florida-Backroads-Travel.com** and let him know. It is his intention to update the book periodically and publish updated editions.

If you have enjoyed this book and read it on Amazon Kindle or purchased a print copy, Mike would appreciate it if you would take a couple of minutes to post a short review at Amazon. Thoughtful reviews help other customers make better buying choices. He reads all of his reviews personally, and each one helps him write better books in the future.

Thanks for your support!

Made in the USA
Columbia, SC
26 May 2018